...AND THEN THERE'S TOMORROW

...And Then There's Tomorrow

ADRIENNE SPRUILL

Adrienne Spruill

Copyright © 2020 by Adrienne Spruill
All rights reserved. No part of this publication may be reproduced, distributed, or transmitted in any form or by any means, without written permission.

Cover design by Adrienne Spruill

Editor: DaVita Miles

First Edition: October 2020

...And Then There's Tomorrow / Adrienne Spruill
ISBN: 978-0-578-77826-6

This book is dedicated to my amazing daughters, granddaughters, family and friends who prayed for me, supported me, listened to me, cried with me, fed me, but most of all you loved me through my good days and held me up through the hard days.

I have had the pleasure to cross paths and befriend many who have more than likely listened to my life slogan: *No matter what everything will be fine. I don't know how and I don't know when, but I promise everything will be okay no matter what happens.*

I must say that I know a little bit about everything and something about nothing as I dare to bare my soul for the world to see. Perhaps in some small measure this book will serve as a reminder that joy exists even in the midst of pain.

~ Adrienne

May your hope and faith be as the frayed feathers in the world that are blown by the wind of uncertainty and still have the audacity to believe it has a purpose in spite of the journey.

~Adrienne

CONTENTS

FOREWORD

INTRODUCTION

1	Wait! What?!	4
2	The Fall and Rise of Wonda' Woman	8
3	First Things First	11
4	Da, Butt!	14
5	Now what!?	16
6	Call me Patches not Peaches	20
7	Choices and Consequences	22
8	Cajun Shrimp Pasta	25

9	Feelings Change	28
10	Soul Pain	32
11	Behind Closed Doors	35
12	Survivorship	39
13	Finding a New Normal	42
14	...And Then There's Tomorrow	46

POSITIVE AFFIRMATIONS

REFLECTIONS

ACKNOWLEDGEMENTS

ABOUT THE AUTHOR

Foreword

Yesterday is the past, today is the present and then there's tomorrow...full of life's good times, bad times and trying times. This book is a compilation of all those times. As I read this wonderful book of candid episodes penned by my cousin, Adrienne, about her breast cancer journey, I gained a new awakening of what it takes to transform from a "Survivor" to a "Thriver!" Every page turned, every chapter completed, I learned so much more about that cute little girl with those extra-long braids who came into my life some 40 years ago! She indeed grew to be the strong one, the humorous one, the patient one, the curious one, the gifted one...the one I bonded with in our family like no other.

As one of the co-survivors who intimately shared in her breast cancer journey, we shared numerous heartfelt telephone conversations since I reside in another town. Through the tone of her voice, I seemingly saw her tears, heard her pain, and felt her heart telling her to never give up Hope...because there is something for her on the other side of tomorrow! I prayed it so, willed it so, and today it is so...my cousin is healed and healthy from breast cancer! I will always remember Adrienne's words to caregivers. In essence she was saying, don't ask if there is anything you can do for someone going through this type of challenge…. just do it! I thank you immensely, cousin!

Finally, those tidbits of wisdom shared at the conclusion of each chapter offer encouragement, strength, love and humor to anyone going through their own personal battles of life.

Never forget to remember that there is always something on the other side of tomorrow!

Dianne E.C. Powell
Founder & Director
Daughter Connection of Hampton Roads, Inc.
(A Breast Health Awareness Non-Profit Organization)

Introduction

Okay, here I am one of the millions and millions of women, men, and children who have become part of a club that we never asked to join. Anyone who has been diagnosed with cancer no matter what form of cancer, are sisters and brothers in this war. As a survivor of cancer, we cannot forget those co-survivors. Co-survivors are the family and friends who go through the journey right by our sides because it takes a village to get through the emotional, physical, and spiritual stress of being diagnosed with a disease.

This isn't a story about a woman struggling with cancer, but rather someone who had the audacity to operate in faith not fear. It's a story of strength, courage, faith, hope and love. May this book in some small manner bless and encourage you along your journey, because trouble doesn't last always. Keep your head up because YOU GOT THIS! No matter what may come your way, IT'S GONNA BE OKAY!

| 1 |

Wait! What?!

December 2015, I am not feeling like myself. Lately I have been sleeping at night holding my left breast for about a month. A small voice in my soul is saying, "go to the doctors and get checked." When I wake up, I'm going to call my gynecologist, and ask for an appointment for a breast examination. As I make my appointment, I think to myself that it's probably nothing. Hopefully I am just over-reacting, but as they say, "it's better to be safe than sorry".

A few days have passed since I made the appointment, and today is the day of my examination. As I sit on the table I am frazzled, and a hot mess. To say I am becoming unhinged is an understatement. I am extremely nervous. Deep in my heart, and in my soul I feel that something could be very wrong.

My gynecologist tries to console me as she checks my left breast for a lump, or a bump. Nothing! She feels nothing on my right breast either. I am due to have my yearly mammogram in February, which is two months away. Despite the results of the check up, I still feel like something is off. In the meantime, I wait with bated breath for February which cannot come soon enough. I continue to hold my left breast on and off. I am not in pain, however that little voice keeps leading me back to the same spot, and I cannot shake it from my psyche.

Christmas comes and goes. January is just one more stepping stone to my mammogram. Finally, it is February, and I am chattier than ever. The technician places each breast one after the other into the mammography machine, which I call the "smasher". If you never had a mammogram, I have to tell you it is an unpleasant experience. You raise one arm against the machine to hold on, trust me you'll want to. The technician lifts your breast, and places it in between two hard plastic plates that smash the breast so the radiologist can take a picture. You have to hold your breath, and try not move any muscles. You swear you are about to faint.

They repeat the process twice, despite the whole mammogram being between 15-30 seconds for each boob, it feels so much longer. After I finish up with the radiologist I hope for the best, and brace for the worst. I am hoping I can laugh this off as just having paid a $25 co-pay to get my boobs smashed and fondled.

A few days pass and finally I receive a call from the radiologist stating that they need to do an ultrasound, because they saw something in my left breast from the mammogram. They want to check a mass they discovered. I was able to get an appointment right away, and went back to radiology. I know something is wrong, because the technician is requesting the radiologist doctor to come into the exam room. I can feel my blood pressure rising quickly as I brace for the worse. The doctor wants me to get a biopsy as a precaution.

I will have to wait a few weeks for the next biopsy appointment. What am I supposed to do until March 4th? How am I not supposed to just give into panic and worry? I try to push back on the notion that something may be wrong, but each day that goes by that little voice in the back of my mind is growing louder and louder. This appointment cannot come soon enough.

After nearly driving myself crazy for the past few weeks, Martin, my significant other, and I are sitting in the waiting room for my biopsy procedure. We don't say anything to each other as I am led into the room to change into my gown. We both know this is serious. So yeah, here I am. Huhhhhhhh. I am alone in this examination room with a random blank stare that's a cross between scared, strong, and hopeful, but deep inside I'm crying without manifesting my tears. I do not know what to expect. I am trying to act normal in an abnormal situation. All I can think to do is nervously make jokes, and keep things light with the doctor. Deep down I know that I am not okay.

The doctor numbs my left breast with a long needle, and proceeds to take samples from the mass. I realize how blessed I am that the radiologists were even able to locate the mass, because the doctor would have never been able to feel the mass during a routine examination.

I watch on the screen as the doctor dives deeper into my breast with a long slender needle attached to a tube-like device. CLICK...CLICK...CLICK. The sound of the machine is actually worse than the procedure. She tells me of her concerns for how deep the mass is located within the tissue, and fears she might not be able to reach it. I watch her tenacity, and determination to obtain a sample from the mass. I continue thanking Jesus for whoever made this numbing cream. CLICK...CLICK...CLICK. She probes deeper into the tissue. The mass is not coming quietly, but her concentration is unwavering. The doctor is finally able to pull samples of this un-welcomed guest from inside my breast. The device continues echoing CLICK..CLICK...CLICK It feels as if time stands still. Thank God she was able to reach it. Phewwww! She took out three samples from the mass, and it is frightening. She leaves a metal marker inside my breast to indicate the area she tested. Finally, it's over, well at least this part of the process. Now the waiting begins, and so do the sleepless nights filled with the anticipation for my pending results.

Word to the Wise: *Be in front of, and not behind life challenges in an effort to make informed choices and decisions. Remember we all have choices in life, and not making any decision at all is also a choice. Don't give up your right to make informed decisions for your well-being and your health. Be proactive in maintaining your health and wellness.*

| 2 |

The Fall and Rise of Wonda' Woman

My kids nicknamed me Wonda' Woman, because like a superhero with infinite strength I am the one who always manages to hold everything together; my household, full time job, my kids, assisting with their school assignments, party planning, and painting in my spare time. I keep the family together; organize all the vacations, cook outs, holiday get together events, cooking, and baking. I am the DO IT ALL or GO TO PERSON. Many of my friends and family wonder how I am able to do so much. If you could pop the top of my head off you would probably find a bunch of mini me's in little cubicles running around like crazy people trying to get it all done. As the reality of this disease begins to set in, Wonda' Woman is wondering how she is going to keep it together.

Today is March 7, 2016, and I get my results from the biopsy. The phone rings, and it's the doctor's office. I rush into another room away from Martin. I press the phone nervously up to my ear. The doctor starts off with, "I'm sorry". She pauses and says, "You have cancer". I feel like I got the air punched out of me, and I can't breathe. I guess I'm not superhuman after all. She continues to talk about the next steps, but all I hear is "you have cancer". The conversation is over as far as I'm concerned. The biopsy confirmed that I have cancer in my left breast. I have cancer. I hang up the telephone, and go to the bathroom. I pick up my towel, and cry into it so I can't be heard. I cry so hard that my head throbs painfully. The doctor's voice keeps replaying in my head. "YOU HAVE CANCER. YOU HAVE CANCER, I'M SORRY." I am in disbelief, and keep replaying it over and over in my head as if I was trying to convince myself of this not being the truth. This must be a dream.

I immediately call Bonnie, my oldest daughter who's a Registered Nurse, and tell her the three most difficult words ever spoken from my mouth - "I HAVE CANCER". I whisper every word. She asks me where I am, and if I told Martin. I say not yet, because I am crying too hard. I didn't want him to hear me. She calms me and says, "Mom, it's going to be okay, we will get through this. Let Martin know."

I wash my face and try to be the superhero everyone knows me to be. I'm always the optimist, but not today. I muster all my strength to tell Martin without breaking down. I last maybe one second after I tell him, and I can't contain myself. I am so broken. I begin to cry uncontrollably. He immediately went into analyst mode grilling me, "When was your last mammogram? Do you get it on time every year?" He calculates the numbers in his head and says, "Everything will be okay! You did everything right; all your appointments were on time. It will be okay."

Wonda' Woman lost her superpowers today, and cancer became my "kryptonite". As I assess my life, I ask the hard questions of, "did

I do everything in life that I set out to do, am I happy, will I survive this?" I had given so much of myself to everyone, and I did not save anything for myself. I recognize that I don't have the strength to do this by myself. I realize my own mortality, and I choose to hold onto life. I have to learn to accept help. Most of all I have to accept the fact that going it alone is no longer an option.

Word to the Wise: *Superpowers are not diminished, because you no longer have physical strength. Strength is an emotional and spiritual part of what makes you strong. Perception may affect your path, and outcome through this journey. Stay positive, and see things as they are not as you wish them to be. Live in your truth. Live in the moment. Live in reality.*

| 3 |

First Things First

First things first, I need to tell my family and friends that I have cancer. I have to prepare myself, because I have no idea how to break the news. I have to make my follow-up doctor appointments. I have to call Mom, Dad, and my brother James "Q Ball". I have to tell my other daughters, DaVita and JaDa, and my granddaughter Antanay. I have to call my closest cousins Dianne, Burnett, and my Aunt Eva. I have to.... I have to just try to calm down, but not right now. I have too many "have to do's" on my to do list. My mind is literally racing.

I contemplate not telling my brother, but Bonnie insists I call him and tell him. I am hesitant to do so, because today is his birthday. What am I going to say, "Hey Happy Birthday I have cancer!" like who does that? I do not want him to hear it from anyone else but me, and I finally find the courage to pick up the phone and tell him. It is as if the air left his body. He is speechless, and somber. My daughter and I tell him we will give him more details later. He sighs and says okay as I hang up, and I dread the next phone call to my Mother.

It is tough telling my Mom. Actually, Bonnie told her and I heard the air leave her body as well. She is a cry baby, and I believe she spent weeks crying. I admit when you think of cancer, you think life is over. To say the least, my Mom thinks my time here on Earth is done. Her Mom died from breast cancer, and to say she is worried for me is an understatement. She finally calms down, and we explain that there are more advances in technology for cancers. Everything is going to be okay. Yep! Fingers crossed.

DaVita, my middle daughter, calls me about my results. She is so much like me, so she could read right through me. She said, "MOM, why are you trying to hide the news from me". I tell her I have cancer. She is living and working in Pennsylvania, and will be moving to Colorado soon. She lets me know she will plan everything around my surgery, and will be staying with me for 3 weeks in Maryland before she moves across country for her new job. She keeps a good front on for me, but I can hear the sadness in her voice. I think she knew I was sick. I always call her, and I wasn't my normal chatty self. She asks if I told JaDa, my youngest daughter, and I say no. She tells me to keep her posted, and I will.

Bonnie decides it would be best to tell JaDa along with Antanay, my granddaughter, together. After Antanay's Honor Society ceremony at school, we all went out to eat. I discover that Bonnie has already told Antanay. We purchase our food and sit down. As Bonnie begins to talk, I knew my baby girl was not okay. She didn't even want her sister to finish the sentence. We didn't even finish our meal. We all walk silently to the car. We try to support each other the best we can, and just cry.

Next, I tell my favorite aunt Eva who is an artist, retired nurse, and is like a second mom to me. My cousin Dianne and I enjoy yearly tea parties and sleepovers with her. We talk and giggle most of the night. Aunt Eva floods me with cards, notes of encouragement, and lots of phone calls. When I break the news to Dianne, she cries so hard. In fact, I believe she cried harder than me. As she sobs to her daughter Natalie, Dianne questions God on "Why Her?". Natalie so eloquently says to her mother, "Mom, why not her?!" Dianne calls me everyday, and fills me with encouragement, support, and prayers. Aunt Eva and Dianne feed my soul.

Cancer has no bias. I have lived my life as a compassionate, and loving person. I go to church, and served as a Sunday School teacher. I love hard and forgive even harder. I have beautiful kids that need me. I have a family that loves me, and friends that I feel so blessed to be a part of my life. I tried to be the best woman I could be, and like to think of myself as a "good person". Cancer doesn't care about any of that. It just is. I have come to accept that the more I live with this disease. I will continue to hold fast to my parents, my brother, and sister (in law) Renata, aunt, cousins, and my closest friends as my rocks. My beautiful daughters, and granddaughters are my superheroes now.

Word to the Wise: *Acceptance is the first step in overcoming difficulties, and when you hit rock bottom you don't have anywhere to go but up. It's okay to not be okay, but always dwell in your truth.*

*As a sidebar I didn't tell too many of my friends as acceptance of this illness proved to be challenging for me. In the midst of it all, I never missed a doctor appointment, or failed to do what was required of me. Always do what's required.

| 4 |

Da, Butt!

The fact that I have claustophobia does not help my cause for all the MRI's and CT scans needed. The doctors informed me that I will need to take a contrast enhanced mammography so they can get good images of my breast. I will have to get an IV contrast, lay on my stomach, place each boob in a hole, and my face into another hole. Then I will be pushed into the MRI machine tube to be scanned.

I explained my issues of feeling closed in small spaces so the doctor gave me a prescription for valium, which was supposed to help me relax during this procedure. Well, in fact the medicine had the opposite effect on me. My eyes were wide open, and heavily dilated. My heart was racing, and to be honest I not only looked crazy, I felt crazy, and I was acting even crazier.

As they call me for my procedure I slowly walk to the room. I look around and remove my shirt and my bra, and put on their gown. The technician places the IV into my arm to prepare for the contrast. Meanwhile, she prepares the MRI machine. I stare at that machine with pure disdain. My personal assessment is that my butt is not going to fit in this machine. I ask the technician if she has something a little bigger. Now, I'm not a big woman, but I'm not a little woman, but if my butt touches this machine I promise her that I will lose it because of my claustrophobia.

The technician requests me to get on my stomach, and place my boobs into each cylinder. Then she requests that I place my face down into the face rest. I hold my hands straight out, and she proceeds to push me into the machine to get me all set up. Well, my gown gets caught when she attempts to pull me out. She takes me out to make adjustments, and then pushes me back into the machine. This time my butt touches the top of the machine, and my gown gets stuck in the machine again.

Now the technician is struggling to pull me out. I am like paper stuck in a copier machine. I am going absolutely nuts! The technician is so frightened she pulls me out, and screams for me to get off the machine. She even removes my IV without realizing it, and orders me to get dressed. I am so angry that I black out, and have gone into some kind of rant scaring the technician. Needless to say, I run out of that office like I am being chased by the law.

Word to the Wise: It's important to express your concerns to hopefully come up with a win-win plan that works for everyone, but I told you several times to not to let the machine touch da butt, right?!

| 5 |

Now what!?

Today is the day of my consultation with the best oncologist and surgeon in the world at Anne Arundel Medical Center. I knew that I might "lose my hearing again", like the first time when they told me I had cancer. Bonnie goes with me to my appointments, and keeps everyone in the loop. There is a lot to remember, and the appointments can be overwhelming so to have her there keeps me on top of everything. The doctors give a lot of statistics, options, choices, etc. It is a lot to take in, and to be honest some of it we didn't understand. We ask a lot of questions. Always ask questions, and be in control of your health and wellness. I cannot express how important it is to make sure you weigh all options, and make the most informed decisions when it comes to your treatment. I know it is cliché, but there is no such thing as a dumb question.

Based on all of the results it is confirmed that I have Stage 1 breast cancer as a result of high levels of estrogen. I decide that the best treatment option for me is a partial mastectomy, chemo, and radiation. The chance of recovery is better than great, and I think the odds are in my favor. After I finish my treatment, I will have to take medication for the next 5-10 years. If I follow the course of action the doctor says, "I will be okay". They set a date for surgery for the partial mastectomy, and I go to my acupuncturist to get rid of some toxins in my body prior to my surgery. I tell the acupuncturist everything, and he is hopeful! I finally feel positive, and empowered. The doctor assigns me a nurse who I refer to as my personal angel. She makes all my appointments, and keeps me on track with everything required in this process.

Today is my surgery. I am going to the Breast Center on the hospital campus to have the radiologist insert a wire into my breast to mark the area for surgery. My Mom, daughters, and granddaughter are in the waiting room. They call me back, and I remove my oversized shirt that Mom gave me. The technician places my breast in the "smasher", and the doctor administers a shot to numb the area. He inserts the wire around the metal marker, and explains that this will be used by the surgeon to remove the section of the cancer in my breast. Believe it or not, although I can see the cancer on the screen it is not visible to the naked eye. It is amazing how something so small can cause such a ruckus.

It is unnerving as I watch the doctor insert the wire, and I have never been so terrified in my life! The technician takes pictures to assure the wire is properly placed around the cancer. The doctor reviews all markers, and makes some minor adjustments to the wire placement to assure that the surgeon is able to remove all of the cancer during surgery. I get dressed, and we all quietly leave so I can check into the hospital.

My family takes turns coming into the room to sit with me before surgery. This is the scariest day of my life, but I continue with a positive attitude laughing with the nurses and doctors. I decide

I want to play a little practical joke on Martin with the help of a nurse. Prior to surgery they request that I take a pregnancy test, and I ask the nurse to announce the test results like they do on the Maury Povich Show. As Martin enters my room, with a smile the nurse says, "we have your pregnancy results, and when it comes to the baby you are," and before she could finish reading the results he says, "it ain't mine. I am not the father." The doctor comes in and we are all in stitches at the pregnancy results, which are negative, of course.

The anesthesiologist comes in and before I know it, I am out. As I wake up, they tell me the surgery is successful! They were able to get every bit of the cancer, including four lymph nodes from under my arm. I do not have to stay overnight, and I am relieved. I am nervous because I didn't know if the cancer spread into my system, or into my lymph nodes. I worry about the unknown, and where to go from here. The first step of my treatment is done, but I know I still have a long journey ahead of me. They place a device in my boob during surgery to maintain the natural look of my breast. You can't even tell that I only have a partial breast. Thankfully, I won't require any surgical breast reconstruction.

I have to come to the realization that I have lost strength. I must depend on others for help, but I am not ready to accept it yet. When all is said and done and as everyone goes home, it is Martin and JaDa left to deal with me and all my shattered pieces. I can't even give myself a shower. I feel bad having to depend on my baby girl through this time travel into unknown territories. I just want to get back to feeling like my old self.

Word to the Wise: *Hope is the gift of miracles. Your attitude matters, and laughter is truly good for the soul. Stay positive no matter what, because you can always find something good in the midst of hard times. I know that what I have experienced and overcame thus far is grace, spiritual and physical healing through mercy, and the love of Jesus Christ. I am the example of what grace looks like, and I am so grateful.*

| 6 |

Call me Patches not Peaches

Let the chemo begin! NOT! Based on the oncologist consultation my hair will fall out after the second round of chemo. My hair is down my back, and has always been a source of pride for me. It is long flowing and curly. I tell JaDa that I will get it all cut off before it starts to fall out. She is devastated and begs me to wait. I honestly never took into consideration that she is going through just as much as I am. She is a co-survivor along with everyone else. I explain to her that if I wake up, and my hair is laying on the pillow it will be so much more devastating to me. My plan is to stay in front of this rather than behind. However, she convinces me to wait and I do. I respect that she needs to mourn, and accept the realization that I have cancer.

Like clockwork I begin to notice my hair coming out as I brush it after my second round of chemo. I put it into a bun so I don't have to deal with it. I am terrified to shampoo my hair, so I don't touch it. The very thought of my hair in my hand terrifies me. I ask JaDa to brush my hair, and put it into a bun for me each morning. She starts to see the hair loss as the days go by. She tells me that is becoming overwhelming and she says, "Mom, it's time". I call my brother James, who is a barber, and let him know that I am ready to cut my hair off.

Sunday he arrives with all his tools, and we have a celebration. My parents, daughters, granddaughter, and my sister (in law) Renata come over. We eat and laugh during my "Bald Head Party". James hesitates, and asks me if I am sure as the clippers quietly buzz. I tell him I accept that this needs to be done. To be honest I don't think he has though. As he cuts the biggest portion of my hair with the clippers, JaDa grabs it and places it into a zip lock bag as a keepsake.

Needless to say, my brother does not cut my hair off bald, but gives me the sexiest haircut ever. It is beautiful. Renata shampoos my hair after my haircut, and some hair rubs away as she rinses it. She tries to cover the spot, but it is not her fault, it is the chemo. LOL. I do not tell her that I know what just happened, but I guess she'll find out after she reads this. She tries to brush it down to cover the patch of missing hair, and this is why I wanted to be bald.

Eventually baldness will be my fate, but for now I will rock this cute haircut as the realization sets in that my hair doesn't define who I am. So call me Patches, for now cause every time I lie down, or scratch I get another patch.

Word to the Wise: *Your hair doesn't define you. True beauty comes from within. So be bald and beautiful!*

| 7 |

Choices and Consequences

So, here's where the drama begins. As if there hasn't been enough so far right? My strength is slowing, and deteriorating much faster than I anticipated. Yet Wonda' Woman still reigns, or at least that's what I want to believe. That's what I am trying to convince myself to believe as truth anyway. Like a numbnut I decide not to get the port placed in my chest for chemo treatment. I have this big plan to do every chemo treatment via IV therapy. Let me tell you, it is not going well for me at all. The nurse is sticking me too many times looking for my vein.

Phew! She finally gets the IV inserted, and begins treatment. After the first bag of chemo medicine is put into my veins the reality, and magnitude of what's happening sets in. This is REAL! It is at this moment that I realize my mortality. Can I survive this? Will I die? Did I do everything in my life that I set out to do? I brace for what will be happen next.

The first bag of medicine finishes, and then the nurse loads up another bag filled with menacing red IV fluid. She tells me that they call it the Red Devil. I watch as the nurse dresses up with a face mask, gloves, and a gown. I ask, "Where is my mask?" as I laugh nervously, but deep down I am scared for my life. She warns that my veins may eventually fail with the IV method for administering the medication versus the port, which was highly recommended. There was so much drama with that nurse locating a good vein, that I made that surgical appointment to get that port inserted before the second round of chemo. I am not going through this again.

A week passes and I am at the hospital, again. The anesthesiologist tells me I may wake up in the middle of port placement and I say, "Oh Lord, I'll be that one to wake up, please don't let me do that. Just hit me in the head with a mallet like on the Fred Flintstone cartoons." Wouldn't you know it was just my luck. Guess who woke up in the midst of surgery, and had a full conversation with the doctor? Yep, me! It was crazy. He lets me know that I am doing great, and he will be finished soon. I let him know he is doing a great job as well.

The doctor says that I was the first patient to ever compliment him in the middle of surgery. Oh, and a shout out to the anesthesiologist. I did not feel one thing! The implantable port is scary, because the placement of the port is under the skin in the chest. At the end of the port is a catheter that sits in a large blood vessel leading to your heart. The most important thing is that this port will allow the nurses to easily administer the medications, and draw my blood. Each time the port and special catheter connect to me to administer the chemo medication it has to break the skin, and leaves two tiny holes. Depending on the day it may or may not hurt a little when it is connected. One thing I know for sure is it does not hurt like the IV needle. That is one positive side to all of this.

Martin drives me to every chemo treatment. Bonnie, my Mom, and brother sit with me every first of the month at the cancer center for my treatments. It is comforting, and an incomprehensible level of support. The cancer center feeds me lunch, and if sandwiches are left over after feeding the other patients, they even feed my family.

During one of my chemo sessions I requested Reiki, which is a Japanese healing technique that channels positive energy through touch to activate the body's natural healing, and emotional well-being. The word Reiki is made of two Japanese words - Rei which means "God's Wisdom or the Higher Power", and Ki which is "life force energy". It is by no means a religion, and does not infringe on your beliefs. I am skeptical, but to be honest it is a spiritual experience. I actually feel the radiance of my energy as the Reiki master massages my legs. It feels warm and calm. I recognize that I did some transfer of energy to her as well, but I don't whisper a word about it to her. As she leaves she thanks me and says, "I came to be a blessing to you, and you blessed me".

Word to the Wise: *In life it's important to be conscious and careful of your life choices. Be it good or bad, there are always consequences for the choices we make in life. Be kind to everyone despite your beliefs and differences, because you never know how you can be a blessing to others or who may be a blessing to you.*

| 8 |

Cajun Shrimp Pasta

After the partial mastectomy I loose mobility, and the use of my left arm due to the removal of 4 lymph nodes. Today, I begin physical therapy to regain my range of motion. I cannot tell you what in the world is going through my head, but I feel good. Despite the sores I have in my mouth from chemo, which makes it painful to eat and drink, I FEEL GOOD! So good in fact that I drive myself to physical therapy. My therapist who is in tune with me is on vacation, and I have someone else to assist me as I work out.

I notice my nails are turning blue. To say I am nervous is definitely an understatement. I tell the therapist, and she does an oxygen check. I am getting enough oxygen. Suddenly I am not feeling so well. The way she is looking at me lets me know I don't look well either. As I leave she says, "be careful going home". I get on the elevator, make a quick stop to the bathroom, and call Bonnie. No answer. I decide to keep moving. I finally have an appetite, and I am sooooo hungry. That small voice says, "sit down," but this time I do not listen.

I enter the garage frustrated with my cell phone, because the WiFi is messing up. I can't get the telephone number to Red Lobster to order some Cajun Shrimp Pasta, my favorite dish. There is no way that I am not going to take advantage of finally wanting to have a bite to eat.

While looking down at my cell phone screen, I suddenly envision myself falling. It is like I am in a dream. I am falling so slow that I actually consider how I want to fall. As time seems to stand still I begin to fall. I cannot fall on my breast, the port, or my bad knee. I turn and try to fall on my butt. My stomach is still growling. I am still falling in slow motion, and thinking OMG when am I going to hit the ground already? What the hell is taking so long? BOOM!!

I don't make around to my butt, but instead land on my stomach and bounce like a skipped rock. I bust my lip on the asphalt. I immediately look up to see where my keys, and cell phone have landed. I look around the garage for someone that could help me, and there was no one. Not one single person.

I'm worried that if I don't get off the ground, I'll get run over. I crawl to get my keys, and cell phone. I force my steps to my car by leaning on every car until I make it to mine. I unlock the door, and put the keys into the ignition so my Bluetooth can connect to my phone. Then everything goes black. The sound of my phone ringing wakes me up, and to my relief it is Bonnie returning my call.

I look around to see where I am after I regain consciousness. I am in my car, the door is open, my left shoe is off, and to say the least I am in disarray. I explain to her that I blacked out, and fell in the garage. She insists that I call 911, and I refuse. I plead for her to come and get me, and take me to the hospital, which by the way is across the street. She makes me call the physical therapy office to let them know I had fallen. I know I will probably become the infamous lady at the office. Everyone will know that I am the one who fell in the garage.

I cannot tell you how I got into my car, and the only answer I have is an angel must have placed me here. Honestly, this whole ordeal lasted only moments, but it feels like hours. Bonnie and Antanay arrive at the garage to pick me up within thirty minutes, and drive me across the street to the hospital.

All I wanted was some Red Lobster Cajun Shrimp Pasta, but now I know that is not going to happen. I am so hungry!

Word to the Wise: *Always listen to that quiet inside voice, because it's always right. Remember you are not an island, and it's okay to need and accept help from others.*

| 9 |

Feelings Change

I am in the ER(Emergency Room) at the hospital with a busted-up leg and lip. They test me for everything, because my immune system is compromised from all the chemo. I am embarrassed, because this all happened due to the fact that I did not want to accept help. I am craving independence more so than ever since my diagnosis. I want to prove that I am strong enough to do something for myself. I should have accepted the ride with Martin. My stinkin' thinkin' landed me here. Most of all, I have been living in a state of denial, and convinced myself that chemo didn't have me, but I had chemo. I was wrong.

The ER doctor comes into the room, and oh my God he is so cute. Anyway, the good news is nothing is broken. The bad news, my knee is busted and is tripled in size. To add insult to injury I cannot walk. It hurts to move so I lay as still as possible. The doctor looks at his notes, and says I will need to remain in the hospital for observation. Then he gives me a look, it is a scornful look, and inches away from my face he begins to reprimand me in front of Bonnie and Antanay. "YOU ARE NOT WELL! YOU

COULD HAVE HURT YOURSELF AND OTHERS! YOU ARE ON CHEMO, AND CANNOT DO THIS ALONE. LET YOUR FAMILY HELP YOU!"

Bonnie and Antanay are glad someone got on me as they constantly scold me, because I rarely ask for help. So long story short, I passed out due to dehydration because I hadn't eaten or drank much over the course of several days due to the sores in my mouth from chemo. Yeah, and I was hungry, really hungry, and well I wasn't going to get my Red Lobster. Not today or tomorrow. I beg the nurse for anything that may be available for me to eat. I was in luck she found one meal of turkey and stuffing, mashed potatoes with gravy, and some vegetables. I relish every bite.

My leg is killing me, and the pain is downright dreadful. I am bedridden, and can't even go to the bathroom by myself. I am peeing in a bed pan, and being wiped like a child by the nurses. The ER doctor asked if I would consider taking morphine to ease the pain. I have never taken morphine, and honestly I am scared. Like am I going to get addicted to this stuff? I start to cry, and the nurse and Bonnie console me. I decide to take it.

I watch the nurse administer the morphine into my IV line. I feel an immediate rush. It is warm and fast moving from the bottom of my feet, through all my veins. When it gets to the top of my head, it feels like my brain is about to explode. It is scary! My mouth tastes funny, and I feel overwhelmed. It is like an outer body experience. I cough. Honestly it did little to ease the pain, and the effects of the drug do not last long. I can see how one could get addicted. I opt to not take the morphine again. I'm allergic to Aleve and Motrin, which reduces swelling in the body, so my only option is Tylenol. That's what I'm sticking with to ease the pain from now on.

They finally get me into a room, and I have to stay for a couple of days. Bonnie and Antanay spend the nights in the hospital right by my side. They get me food from the cafeteria. Len, Bonnie's dad, comes to visit me the very next morning. Martin arrives later in the evening. As the days go by the nurse eventually force me out of the bed to take myself to the bathroom. I am told that I will be released. Unfortunately, my leg is so swollen that the hospital does not have a brace large enough for it. I wish they did it would give me the much needed support. They suggest I purchase a walker, or a cane to get around the house. I struggle to get out of the hospital bed, and go to the bathroom to get dressed. I am in pain, but happy to use the toilet instead of the bed pan.

As I am wheeled to the garage for my ride home, I laugh about the doctor and how cute he was. I thought I was looking good, and it turns out I have hairdo drama. As a matter of fact I am looking crazy. Bonnie didn't have the heart to tell me I look a hot mess. Antanay takes a picture of my patchy head, and texts it to JaDa who has absolutely no filter. JaDa sends me the picture, and texts, "Mom, put your hat on." Turns out that the hospital pillow had rubbed all my hair out in the back. LOL. I just have to laugh at myself shaking my head.

I struggle to get into the car to go home, and realize driving is not an option for quite a while. Martin picks up my car from the garage, and drives it home. I guess you could say God saved me from myself.

Moral of the story is, "check yourself before you wreck yourself". I am so thankful I didn't hurt anyone, including myself. When you aren't in the right frame of mind, it's important to depend on those around you to help you make good decisions. It took months before I was able to walk or drive again. I am so thankful, because things could have ended much worse.

Word to the Wise: *Don't be led by your feelings, because they change from moment to moment. Don't get screwed up by the picture that's in your head - that's not real. Live in your truth, and the reality of each moment.*

| 10 |

Soul Pain

I continue to get weaker and weaker by the minute. Chemotherapy is taking a big ole fat chunk out of me. I have lost one toe nail, all my fingernails and toenails are brittle, and lifting off while growing new nails at the same time. I keep my nails trimmed low. A little bit of good news is that I am nearing the end of chemo, however radiation will be starting soon. I wish I didn't rock the sexy hairdo and the patches in my hair, because now the hair follicles have become brittle and hard. The next time I get a hair cut it's painful. My follicles are like tiny sharp daggers. Lesson learned it's best if you just cut all the hair off the first time around.

I develop neuropathy in both my feet from the chemo so walking has become painful. It's like walking on pins and needles. DaVita is home to assist with my care before moving to Colorado. I am nearing the end of my last weeks of chemo, and this new round of medicine knocked me to my knees. I am in so much pain that I feel it in the core of my soul. I want to give up the ghost right here and now, but I can't. I think about everything that I have done in my life, my kids, my granddaughter, and my new granddaughter who will be born soon. DaVita watches helplessly as the color leaves my face. She rubs my feet, prays for me, and slowly closes the door to my bedroom. I do not wish this pain on my worst enemy. I lay here quietly, and suffer in silence. I don't even have tears left to cry. When I finally manage to release one single tear, I remain still so I won't disturb the pain.

I am going through a metamorphosis as I spin a web around my emotions. I am becoming a recluse, and tuck myself away in the spare room to not be a burden on anyone. It is also a safe space to hide my pain. I do not like who I am becoming. I don't like how I feel. I just lay here day in and day out in complete silence, and numb to every emotion as I wait for the pain to pass.

Today is my last chemo treatment, and I am grateful that this is over. An unexpected side effect of the chemo is what the doctor call "chemo brain", which is memory impairment caused by the treatment. Often, I have trouble expressing myself, because I can't remember words. Words that I know, that I use everyday. I am at a loss for words, and incredibly frustrated. The one thing I know for sure is that I am frightened. I don't know how my body is reacting to all that has happened so far, what is currently taking place, and what tomorrow will look like for me.

Radiation begins soon after chemo, and to be honest it isn't as bad as chemo. It definitely is scary, because you have to be completely still as high doses of radiation is precisely delivered to kill the cancer cells in your body. The radiation department plays great music. All the 80's and 90's music. As the machine hums and circles my body I focus on the songs, and just sing in my head. I keep my eyes shut, and try to disregard the metallic monstrosity that circles my body. I am too afraid to even breathe as radiation is delivered close to my heart.

Thankfully, I did not burn until the last couple of treatments, and oh boy that is some crazy pain. All the skin under my breast is burned off all the way down to the white meat. I keep the area clean, dry, and apply ointments to prevent infection and promote healing. It is a lot to do, but it is definitely a necessary part of the process. I am so grateful to those doctors who delivered the radiation treatments. The only thing I can equate radiation to is being rotisseried like a chicken. Radiation is the last step to target and kill any remaining cancerous cells.

Word to the Wise: *Sometimes you need to be alone, but don't believe the things you tell yourself when you are hurting or in pain. Speak life to yourself, because the universe is listening to your every word. Brighter days are coming. I promise!*

| 11 |

Behind Closed Doors

Grief comes in 6 stages for me: denial, isolation, anger, bargaining, depression, and acceptance. I believe each individual stage bears its own cross based on your personal experience.

I was not in denial about the cancer diagnosis, I was in disbelief. I was not even in denial about how sick I really was when I was going through chemo and radiation. I was in denial that I needed help. I was in denial that I could no longer do normal things like clean, cook, drive, walk the dog, and take a shower without assistance. The realization of needing help did not hit me until I fainted in the garage, and the doctor scolded me. I could have seriously injured myself or even worse someone else, because I wanted to prove that I was even stronger than before. I wanted to prove that I could take care of my needs, yet I was helpless and felt useless. I understand the meaning of not taking the little things in life for granted, and to "stop to smell the roses".

In my isolation chambers, which was the spare room, I tuck myself away from sunrise to sunset and from everything and everybody. I do not want any physical contact with anyone. I don't want to be asked, "How are you feeling? Are you alright? or Do you need anything?" You can't even imagine how I feel, which is beyond horrible. You know that I am not okay. I don't know what I want. And I don't know what tomorrow will look like for me.

I stare into infinity. There is no television, no phone, just quiet. I listen to the sound of nothing. I hate who I have become. I was that laugh out loud, an animated woman who made people smile and laugh uncontrollably. I cannot find anything to smile about right now, but I am grateful to be alive. I am angry, angry at cancer because I have no control of this situation. I don't get to make the rules. I don't get to determine the outcome.

I don't bargain with God. I am not angry with God. However, I realize that I am bargaining with myself. This is my first line of defense in postponing my grief, anger, sadness, and vulnerability. I want my positive mental attitude to return, and dream of future where I am cancer free. I think to myself, there has to be some deeper meaning to why this is happening to me. I want to be healthy, live a happy life, and enjoy my family. I want to be here for all my kids "aha" life moments. I want to make cookies with my grandkids, and shower them with love and kisses. I want to regain control of me. My life that once was is nowhere to be found at this particular moment.

I can honestly say that I am extremely depressed. I'm not sure if it is the medicine, or just the reality of it all - perhaps a combination of all things internal and external. My emotional and mental health is questionable. I don't even have the strength or desire to take a shower, brush my teeth, or even eat. The mood swings are a roller coaster ride. I cry for no reason, and laugh uncontrollably, which is good for the soul. Nonetheless I have become a recluse, a depressed, and stinky recluse. I'm not even sure if anyone is aware of this, because I smile through the pain so no one will worry about me. Martin remains his calm self. He makes dinner for JaDa and me, and watches television. He won't get on the roller coaster ride with me, and I am grateful that he gives me room to deal with my emotions. He never judges or patronizes me, and allows me to figure it all out on my own terms.

Acceptance comes at a high cost. I know I keep mentioning this, but the thought that I risked everyone's safety, including my own after that fall in the garage still bothers me. That fall saved my life, because I was no longer able to drive or walk. I was forced to sit down, relax, reflect, and regain my strength. I want to be okay so bad, and prove my independence. I never had anything to prove. My friends and family were always there for me. They support and love me. I am the one with the issue. I have to accept the way things are at this moment, get through the process of change, and put things in perspective. I have to change what I am able to change, and accept what I cannot. Denial is no longer an option.

As I reflect on all that has happened as I complete my chemo and radiation treatments, and walk over to ring the ceremonial to let everyone know I completed my treatment at the cancer facility. I ring that bell until my arm is tired. The joy of completing my treatment is something I cannot explain. That bell is the ultimate symbolism of hope for beginning, and a cancer free life. This time is also filled with many uncertainties for whether or not I am truly cancer-free or will remain cancer-free.

I don't feel sorry for myself, but I am very angry. I am angry as hell, which has chipped away pieces of my soul. As the Bible says it's okay to be angry, but just don't sin. In other words, it's okay to be angry, but be careful what you do with that anger when you are going through. I realize that this is my fight, and yes, I will fight this disease. It will not win! God willing it will not win. It has taken me a while to accept this illness, to say out loud, "My name is Adrienne and I am a cancer survivor".

So, if I may suggest that if a co-survivor wants to be a blessing to the survivor avoid asking if the survivor needs anything, or how they feel. We don't want to be a burden despite the fact that we are not being a burden. Therefore, we will more than likely not ask for help. A simple card, gift basket, prayer, a ride to doctor appointments, grocery shopping for us, or a prepared meal is a welcomed surprise.

Word to the Wise: *GET OUT OF SURVIVAL MODE. It's a new day. Set yourself free, and allow yourself to live and thrive. Forgive and let go of any anger you may hold for yourself, or others so you can move on with your life.*

Change is not necessarily bad, however it can be really uncomfortable. Embrace change with an open mind and heart. Consider change as a different way of doing things, and transform into the new you with love and joy rather than fear and anger.

Take time to enjoy the beauty of life. Take time to smell the roses.

| 12 |

Survivorship

There is a lot of buzz around survivorship. It's not just about being a survivor, but also a thriver. The National Cancer Institute defines survivorship as the "focus on the health and life of a person with cancer post treatment until the end of life. It includes the physical, psychosocial, and economic issues of cancer, beyond the diagnosis and treatment phases."

Survivorship includes; the cancer survivor, co-survivors, and anyone who is a part of the care giving process. It is a shared experience that touches every family member, friend, and caregiver. It is an important part of the process as you go through cancer treatment, and living beyond the diagnosis. It's about living life to its fullest.

I will be honest my relationships with everyone changed. Some for the better, and some for the worst. Most of all I changed. Change is often scary, because you just don't know the outcome. My youngest daughter, JaDa is the youngest co-survivor in my life. She is quite strong, and often does not share her emotions. She is starting high school, and as a result of all the changes it is overwhelming. The uncertainties of my health have caused her to become distant, bitter, and mean towards me. The irony of it all is that I was finally accepting help from everyone, and it never even dawned on me how she felt.

I eventually found out that she was scared and jealous of the Mom her older sisters had. She felt that she may not have the pleasure to enjoy time with me in the same manner as her sisters, because of my health. I needed and accepted JaDa's help with showers, and getting dressed, but now I feel horrible. I put too much stress on her, and never once considered how she felt. I get it. She hated what the cancer had done to me, and the transformation from Mom with superpowers to powerless Mom. She witnessed my deterioration, and metamorphosis firsthand. She wondered whether or not I would be there for the important moments of her life. I hated that she had to see me like this, and secretly I was scared too.

We all have our breaking points. I get it. I tried to talk to her, but she wasn't listening. She couldn't hear me, or maybe I just couldn't express myself. I ask Bonnie to speak with her and calm her fears, and as a result our relationship became even stronger.

The ordeal with Jada was a real eye opener. I was outside of my comfort zone, and it enabled me to get back pieces of my life. From this day forward I will shower and dress myself, which is not only empowering, but feels so good.

Word to the Wise: *It's important to recognize your co-survivors, and be aware of their feelings. They are hurting too! The power of hope can change your life, but so does an open line of communication. Sometimes* *you have to walk in another persons shoes to understand what they may be feeling.*

| 13 |

Finding a New Normal

I cannot tell you what a new normal will look like. All I know is that I am not the same person. I try to reach out for the old me, but I just cannot find her. I want the old me to return, but the reality is she does not exist anymore. As I complete my transformation and metamorphosis the old me is only a memory. I am emotionally, spiritually, and mentally a different person. My hope is that this experience will change me for the better.

My brother takes me back to the hospital to have my port removed from my chest. It is liberating as it represents freedom from the process of cancer treatment. It takes only 15 minutes for the surgery. The pain is bittersweet, because the port was my lifeline for my medication and my way to get better. On the other hand I worry if whether or not I will need it later. Like what if I have a relapse. For now I will believe that I am healed in Jesus name.

I ask for pain medicine, which just so happens to be the same medication that I have in my purse. It takes too long for the effects to kick in. I ask for something stronger, but they have no open beds to administer a stronger pain medicine, and the wait time is 2 hours. I want to go home so I will just take this pill, so they can release me from the hospital. I'm ready to go home now!

To celebrate my brother and I grab a bite to eat at Ms. Shirley's, a restaurant in downtown Annapolis, Maryland. He worries that I do not eat enough, and orders way too much food. As we are eating the medicine finally kicks in as my laughter turns into a silent stare. I am about to go to sleep. My brother quickly pays the check, and drags me all the way to the car so he can take me home. It is hilarious! I am so loopy! I sleep all the way home. Once I get into the house I sleep for several more hours.

The port removal is liberating and symbolizes the end and beginning for me. I look into the mirror, and I look sick. I don't feel sick, but I look different. My breast is numb from the partial mastectomy and lymph node removals. I am afraid to touch my breast or wash it when I shower. So, I squeeze soap over it, and let the water just roll down my chest until all the soap is gone. It hurts to walk, because of the neuropathy. My toenail hasn't grown back yet. All my nails which turned black from the chemo are finally starting to lighten.

My once beautiful smooth skin is a bumpy mess. My cheeks are rosy red from all the chemo and medications. My long beautiful hair is now a crazy tuff of something on the top of my head. I do not like wigs. I tried them out, but to be honest they are just too hot to wear. It feels like I have a pair of tight underwear on my head. I opt for a nice hat or scarf instead while I wait for my hair to grow back.

I have to use a paraben and aluminum free deodorant. I try every deodorant at the drugstore and grocery store. I quickly discover that they do not provide me with odor protection. It takes me about a year to find something that I love, and I recommend it to my family and friends.

The last thing I notice, and I don't know how I didn't notice this immediately is that I have no FRICKING EYEBROWS! Oh, my goodness. I laugh uncontrollably, and use the eyeliner pencil to draw my eyebrows in surprised looks for fun.

As I reflect on everything that has happened, I am so grateful that: treatment is over, my burned boob from radiation is beginning to heal, my skin is returning, my hair is starting to grow back, my toenail is growing back, my eyebrows however are not growing back to their full thickness. I continue to draw a line for my eyebrows, and I may actually get my eyebrows tattooed.

Laughter is truly the best medicine, and I encourage you to always find a reason to laugh. Finding a new normal is scary. Although I am not sure who I am anymore, I have never felt more alive. It is like meeting a person for the first time, and learning all about them. All those emotions you feel are real, so don't ignore them, but rather relish in the opportunity to perhaps become a better version of yourself.

I don't get consumed by the "would of, could of, or should of". This experience by all means may have an impact on your spiritual, emotional, physical, and even cause sexual challenges. Embrace your new normal with an open mind, and dare to be an even better person than before. Don't be afraid to become a new and improved version of you!

Word to the Wise: *Find pleasure in the little things. Stay away from negative and unhappy people. It's important to keep your stress to minimum levels, the ultimate goal is no stress, but life happens. Although there may be fear of the possibility that this cancer may return, or whatever sickness that may come, it's important that we continue to be faithful, encouraged, and believe everything will work out for the good.*

Press forward and live your best life now. It's a new day!

| 14 |

...And Then There's Tomorrow

It has been a long road to recovery. Difficult times give you character, and experience that can be used to help others. I have gained a deeper respect, knowledge, and wisdom that has breathed new life into me. I have opened the door for possibilities that were unknown. I learned the importance of maintaining a positive attitude despite it all, and the faith to press on in spite of how things appeared.

You can look at the glass half empty or half full. I always say the glass is full, because if I pour into a shorter versus taller glass, then the glass is always full. Surround yourself with family and friends that love, support, and pray with and for you and with you. Declare your healing, and deliverance! It won't come when you want it, but God is always on time. I haven't arrived, but I am going to keep it moving.

Today has its challenges. I had to learn how to use my arm, and how to do things we take for granted, such as taking off and putting on my clothes. I developed other health challenges, but then there is tomorrow filled with new hopes, dreams, and opportunities. You have another chance for joy, happiness, and healing. Another chance to get it right. Another chance to make a difference in the world.

Prayer still works. This to shall pass. The storm doesn't last always, and then there's tomorrow. Trust in the Lord with all your heart, and lean not unto your own understanding. In all your ways acknowledge Him, and He shall direct your paths. (Proverbs 3:5-6)

Stay positive, and make affirmations that feed your soul. Remember the powers of life and death are in your tongue, and the universe is always listening to you. Always speak life, and be blessed in all you do. Tomorrow is another opportunity for you to be better than today.

POSITIVE AFFIRMATIONS

♥ Meditate! Let your mind and body work in harmony.

♥ Speak life and positive affirmations out loud. Let the universe hear you!

♥ Speak to yourself in third person, if necessary. Speak to your soul.

♥ Remember, YOU are a warrior!

♥ Look for brighter days, push through the pain, and weather the storm because on the other side of the storm is where the sunshine awaits you.

♥ Choose a theme song, turn the music up loud, and sing your heart out whenever you feel down in the dumps.

♥ Happiness is a choice. Oh, but joy is what you seek!

♥ Accept the reality of your illness and allow your family and friends to assist you.

♥ Trust that God will bring you through and that your experience will be used to help others.

♥ Find an aluminum and paraben free deodorant that doesn't make you stink.

♥ When you look good, you feel good. Do something special for you.

♥ Laughter has been proven by doctors to be the best medicine as it releases the body's natural feel good chemicals. So laugh in abundance.

♥ Lose the upside-down smile (frown). If necessary, have a 60 second pity party. You are only allowed one a day.

♥ Being hopeless is not the same as being helpless. Hopelessness drains the soul. It's important to keep hope alive. I encourage you to keep the faith despite how things appear.

♥ Trust that God will bring you through, and that your experience will be used to help others.

♥ Dry your eyes, smile, then carry on with your day because: YOU GOT THIS!

Reflections

"I was devastated and scared for my daughter, and scared that cancer would happen to me. I cried and cried and cried. I went with my daughter to every chemo treatment to hold her hand. I remember looking at hats, and scarves with her at the cancer center. I am so happy it's over, and that she has been four years cancer free." ~Mom

"You feelin' okay? You need anything? You need me to do anything? Alright, you okay? You sure?"   ~Dad's daily telephone conversations

"Just checkin' on you. Did you eat today? Get some rest." ~Qball's daily telephone conversations

"Initially I was shocked, and didn't really know what to think or how to feel. I just knew I had to be strong for my Mom. The nurse in me kicked at every appointment for chemo. I was there not only for support, but making sure things were done correctly. I wanted no mistakes when it came to my Mom. She always had a poker face on; but I know her. She was scared, and I just wanted her to know she didn't have to hide her fear, because I'd be there every step of the way as her warrior." ~Bonnie

"Sitting in the corner of the classroom in disbelief, many questions running through my head. Why my Grandmother? Why somebody who is nothing but good to the world? WHY? Moments later I find myself in the school bathroom crying, thinking of the unbelievable...the good..the bad. After conversations with my Mom, I was told to set my emotions aside to physically be there for my Grandmother. At almost every chemo session keeping my composure..cracking jokes to turn frowns upside down. Keeping a positive mindset, because she is a SURVIVOR! ~Antanay

"When my Mom got cancer I continued to work. I lived as though I wouldn't lose her. Thank God for some good friends that helped me come to grips with my emotions. Cheraine who had beat her cancer, and Lindsey whose Mom fought and won her battle; those ladies are rock stars. When my Mom fainted in the parking garage that was when reality set in. Bald head and busted bruised lips all purple, and scabby my Mom still smiled and played it off. Damn that's courage. I cut her hair once, and I will never forget the small black tuffs of hair falling to the cold white tiles of the kitchen floor. The clippers overheated in my hand, because I was so nervous it took me longer than I expected to shave her. Given the state of my dog's last cut I wasn't sure why she trusted me, but she coached me all the way on how to do it properly. She used to cut hair, and I don't think she would have ever imagined being on the opposite end of that chair.

I am grateful that I still have her in my life. I know I am blessed, and extremely lucky. I still fuss at her to take it easy, and she reminds me to do the same. We have each other's backs in that way. I love her, and if she didn't know it before she's special." ~DaVita

"When I found out that my Mom was diagnosed with cancer, we were coming from my niece's honor roll ceremony, and I remember us walking to the car laughing and giggling. Then we got to the car, and we were still in the parking lot at her school. We were sitting in silence. My older sister, my niece, and my Mom were all giving each other that look like we should tell her now, and the silence was broken. My Mom said, "Jay I have to tell you something, and I don't want you to be upset". I started thinking like what would I be mad or upset about, and then she said, "I have breast cancer", and I got quiet. After a couple seconds I said "okay, you will be fine, because you're a fighter". Then I asked if we could go to Chick-Fil-A. No one knew, but deep down I was hurt. I didn't want my Mom to die from this disease. So, as my Mom was getting treated for cancer, I was angry and upset that this was happening. Even though I was angry, and upset I stood by my Mom because I was the one living at home with her; watching, bathing her, feeding her, keeping her spirit up even when mine was down. All in all, I was making sure my Mom was okay. The thing with cancer is it doesn't only affect the person that has it, but it affects the people around that person, because you don't want to see your love ones hurt or feel that pain. If there's someone out there that's supporting a love one with cancer, and is bottling up their anger, don't be afraid to talk about it with that person or anyone." ~JaDa

"God wouldn't give you a burden too heavy to carry. In other words, anything that you go through isn't enough to break you or stop you from being the strong human being that you are. God gives his toughest battles to the strongest people. Whatever you're going through, understand that it doesn't last forever. You decide how you feel within yourself. Think positive, and bring light to any terrible situation you're in. You create your reality. If there is a void, choose to fill it with joy." ~Angela

"Adrienne, my adopted daughter and friend. I am so pleased that I have had the pleasure to see you grow up from the photo that your parents sent to us in Illinois when you were a toddler. I have always been delighted to see your talent from crafts to art. You are a special light to our family. Your smile, your joy, your humor, your kindness, thoughtfulness is a delight for the family. God made you special for a reason. He gives each of us the personality we will need to overcome the times when life is not what we plan. Keep looking forward. Yesterday is finished. The future has not come yet. Live in the present moment. May you be filled with peace, joy, love and light, and may the Light of Truth Overcome All Darkness! ~Om Shanti" ~Eva Maria

"Adrienne Spruill, my wonderful cousin, has been cheerful, upbeat, helpful and thoughtful from the time she was a little girl to now as an adult mother. I have seen her practice the qualities of courage, persistence, and confidence. I know she daily uses these qualities to succeed in life, and to stay strong in her life, journey. I am very glad to be a witness to her ability to grow in her self-development. I am proud to be a part of the family." ~Blessings. W. Michael Cox

"I want to reflect on my sister in law, who is more like my sister. When I found out you had breast cancer, I was speechless and hurt. I remember crying on my way to work. I call her Fathead, and I told her we will get through this. So many family members depend on her, and I knew this was going to be a challenging situation for her and the family. But you know she always made everyone feel reassured that she was okay. I knew in my heart she was getting tired, but she kept pushing until the day she was cured. I remember the day when my girls and I went to visit her to cheer her up. We went to the restaurant to have dinner, and she would have us cracking up about some wild experience with her body changes. I am so grateful to have a sister like her, you are so beautiful inside and out. Sis keep striving to do your best. God made you a stronger and wiser women, and yes you did it. ~Love, Renata

"I was shocked, concerned, worried, but knowing how God loves us and could heal you. I was very hopeful, and not doubtful you'd be okay with family and friends' support. Having and reading Gods word I knew how strong you are, but trusted and believed that Diva would be okay." ~Charlotte

"When you called and I found out you were sick and had cancer, I panicked without you knowing. In that moment, I decided to be strong for you to lean on me. What I didn't know was you were a warrior the whole time. I would call you to see how you were doing, while hanging on the edge, but you always stayed true to yourself. Always laughing and with a positive attitude, and in good spirits. I know it wasn't easy, but I knew you cut your hair with acceptance of knowing your hair would grow back more beautiful than before. I would look at you, like girl here it is everybody our age is losing hair and here you are with this new found growth, just gorgeous. I am so grateful you are well, and like the rest of us, healthier enough to continue fighting another day. Celebrating you and thankful you are my forever beautiful friend, Age. Love you Lady." ~Alicia

Title: "A Walk of Courage and Hope"
"Whilst Adrienne was fighting the good fight against such an unforgiving disease, she did not allow it, in any capacity, to change her attitude. Yes, there were hard days. Fear. Trepidation. Anger. Sadness. However, these

feelings were out numbered in groves by Resolve. Bravery. Valor. Heart. Adrienne showed her half glass full of spirit and attitude. Her most appreciated humor was just as present as before the diagnosis. She made it okay for us to support her through. She walked with courage and hope; God guiding her every step of the way. Whew. Thank you oh Great Spirit."
~Crazy Curley (aka Annette Gertrude Curley)

"Well nothing is more hurtful than to hear your friend and someone you look up to faced with cancer. My heart was in disbelief, skipped a beat, and tears fell. Something about hearing it from the person themselves is a little bit more intimate and captures the soul with more impact than to hear it from someone else. As I was told it was the sadness of what she went through that was heart breaking. However, it was the overwhelming feeling of joy to know she was standing and here at this moment. This was a moment of triumph for all the trials. She can continue to keep sharing a lifetime of memories with me and others. You can forget the cancer and wish it goes to hell and love on the person because you realize how short life is for anyone." ~Khalilah

"Quote:"Learning is a Gift even when Pain is your Teacher"
To Adrienne, My Lucille Ball, My Carol Burnett, My Friend. One word that means the most to me when I think of you is Love. Your Love of Family, Your Love of God, and Love you show to Friends. Additionally, your Strength to Overcome all challenges that come your way is beyond comprehension. Whatever lies ahead, know you'll have the love and support of many to get you to your Goal. ~Love Always, Tony

Acknowledgements

I want to thank my parents, my brother, my sister (in law), my beautiful daughters and granddaughters, Aunt Eva, cousin Mike, cousin Dianne and family, cousin Burnett, and Martin for the love and support through one of the most difficult times of my life. I would be amiss if I did not acknowledge all my co-survivors and closest friends who I've had the pleasure to be part of my life for over 20 years.

A special thanks to my co-workers that have become part of my family, and some who gifted me with perfume and eyeliners, joined me in my celebrations of life in the midst of this illness, called me frequently, sent me cards and texts, but most of all prayed for me. You all have been my rock, and I thank you from the bottom of my heart for the love and support that was ever so evident by each of your actions.

May you be blessed and have the fortune to be a blessing to someone else along this journey called Life.

"Hope is never deferred. Make the impossible possible with good intentions – speak it, think it, and live it. Even if your hopes don't materialize into reality this day remember… then there's tomorrow.

May your faith be the guide through your darkest times and hope the lantern of light that is never deferred."

~Adrienne

...And Then There's Tomorrow

About The Author

Born and raised in Washington, D.C., Adrienne Spruill attended Howard University (Major: Human Ecology), Prince George's Community College (Major: Art), and went on to graduate from University of Maryland University College (UMUC) with a Bachelor of Science Degree in Marketing. She holds a District of Columbia Instructor License in Barbering and a Cosmetology License. She has been cancer free since 2016 and uses her voice to encourage and empower all who cross her path.

www.ingramcontent.com/pod-product-compliance
Lightning Source LLC
Chambersburg PA
CBHW070303010526
44108CB00039B/1811